SOCIAL ANXIETY

Think differently, Talk Wisely, and Influence People.

LAKSHMI SAGAR G

DEDICATION

The book **"SOCIAL ANXIETY"** is dedicated to readers struggling to face the fear of people. I personally thank my aunt and uncle, my parents, my teachers, my brothers, my close ones, and my friends.

Copyright

About Author

Lakshmi Sagar G is currently pursuing a Ph.D. in Physics. He draws inspiration from renowned self-help authors. His passion for reading these influential thinkers fueled his interest in writing, which he began developing during his college years.

In 2017, driven by a desire to inspire and uplift others, he launched his motivational website aimed at helping individuals achieve their goals. Over the years, he has cultivated extensive blogging experience, particularly crafting short motivational articles. His writing focuses on work motivation, goal setting, productivity, overcoming procrastination, resilience in the face of failure, and pursuing dreams. His articles have gained widespread popularity on platforms like Reddit, where readers appreciate his relatable and encouraging insights. Lakshmi Sagar G's primary aim is to motivate and guide people toward building fulfilling and successful lives.

As a self-published author, he has released several works on platforms such as Amazon, Google Play, Notion Press, and Draft2Digital. His ebooks have reached an impressive milestone, with over three lakh copies downloads across platforms like Google Play Books and Amazon. His work has received thousands of positive reviews from readers, attesting to the impact his writing has had on their lives.

Below, you will find glowing reviews that reflect readers' value in his motivational guidance.

Reviews from readers of the author's previous books

Anirban Sadhukhan

★★★★★ July 5, 2023

After a one month depression . i have the igonorance from my dearest one but she didnot come towrds me in that time . i always think about her . and it is the cause of my depressed . i forget to live alive in that time . Now these lessons motivate me and give me a great path thank you sir . thank you for your help

Did you find this helpful?　　Yes　　No

sedney ziah

★★★★★ August 10, 2024

I always felt soo uneasy then 1 night I saw this and decided to read it. it makes me cry then I got good sleep because of this I always can't sleep peacefully because of this uneasy feeling that I don't know the reason I just let it out by crying and listen to calm music then read thisss it's all worth it!!

Monika Gupta

★★★★★ July 21, 2024

Honestly speaking I loved this book and I am gonna read this e-book everyday to not forget the things I read in it. Worth reading it will only take your 30-45 minutes. Go and read it man

Did you find this helpful?　　Yes　　No

Nikhil KUMAR

★★★★★ April 10, 2023

well thoughts of the book are real and true which makes me to become a worm of reading I just try to reading one more chapter out of the readings I read in a day from this book and yes You said well that"CRICTICS ARE THE LADDERS TO BUILD YOUR PERSONALITY"you perform it well 🙏 🙏 🙏 🙏 🙏 🙏 🙏 🙏 🙏 🙏 🙏 . THANYOU SO LAKSMISAGAR JI FOR THIS BOOK AND I HOPE I YOU PROVIDE MORE BOOKS FOR LEADING US FROM DARKNEES TO LIGHT . THANK YOU SO MUCH.

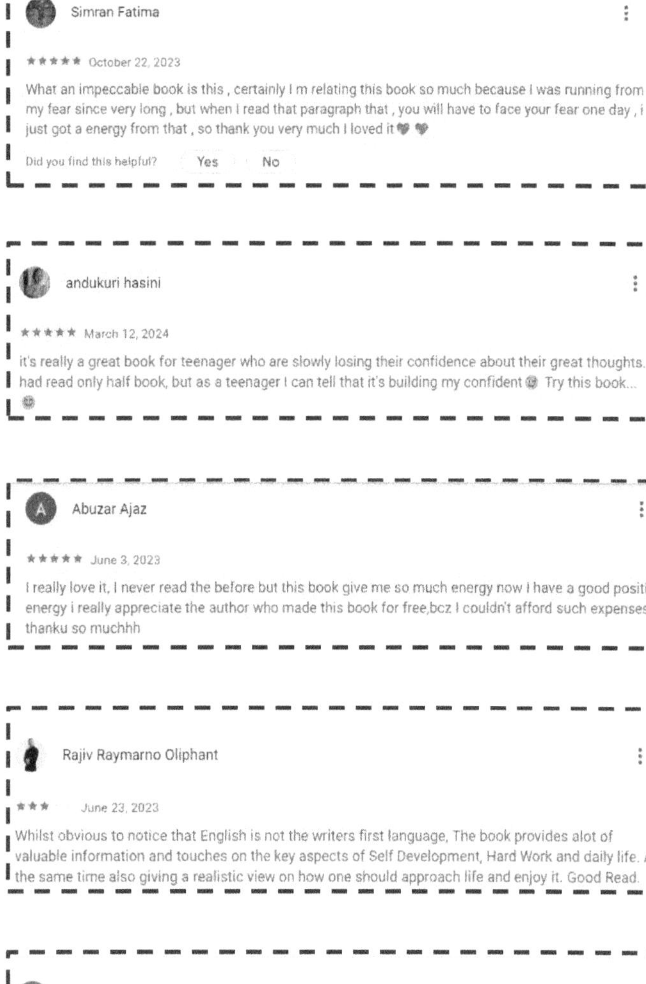

Simran Fatima

★★★★★ October 22, 2023

What an impeccable book is this , certainly I m relating this book so much because I was running from my fear since very long , but when I read that paragraph that , you will have to face your fear one day , i just got a energy from that , so thank you very much I loved it 🖤 🖤

Did you find this helpful?   Yes   No

andukuri hasini

★★★★★ March 12, 2024

it's really a great book for teenager who are slowly losing their confidence about their great thoughts. I had read only half book, but as a teenager I can tell that it's building my confident 😊 Try this book...
😊

Abuzar Ajaz

★★★★★ June 3, 2023

I really love it, I never read the before but this book give me so much energy now I have a good positive energy i really appreciate the author who made this book for free,bcz I couldn't afford such expenses, thanku so muchhh

Rajiv Raymarno Oliphant

★★★   June 23, 2023

Whilst obvious to notice that English is not the writers first language, The book provides alot of valuable information and touches on the key aspects of Self Development, Hard Work and daily life. At the same time also giving a realistic view on how one should approach life and enjoy it. Good Read.

Olebogeng Mokwena

★★★★   February 17, 2024

I just finished reading the book and it's a great book. I look forward to applying the lessons in my reality. The English used in the book book can be improved but I liked it 👍

Did you find this helpful?   Yes   No

Ada walking Emils

★★★★ August 31, 2023

This book has taught me at least over 6 lessons that I myself have never even heard of before. The lessons in this book has improved my life to the extent that I feel more calm and the changes within my lifestyle. Overall, I recommend this book if you need a dozen or 2 lessons for life.

Did you find this helpful?   Yes   No

Anshu Kashyap

★★★★ July 23, 2023

every lines are most power full. Its full of positive lines. fully motivational book. mind-blowing line 👍 😊

Did you find this helpful?   Yes   No

Iene chio

★★★★★ October 28, 2023

I really love how genuine the writer to his readers. All the best!

Did you find this helpful?   Yes   No

Sudesh

★★★★★ June 29, 2023

I have no words about this amazing book. I am so glad to get this chance to develop myself. The quotes of this book is really mind boggling and change my thoughts about life. I thankful to the narrator of this book. I think this is very good opportunity for youngster's coz this life changing book is free of cost. I am very grateful to get a chance to change my thoughts about life with the help of this book so, this is the reason, I gave five out of five to this book. Hats'of 👍

Did you find this helpful?   Yes   No

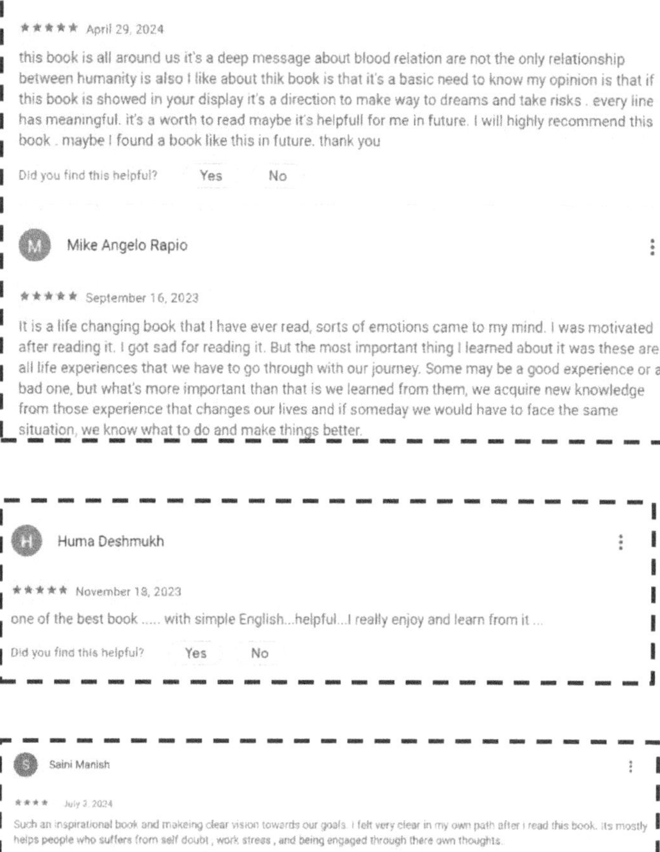

A   Asad Malik

★ ★ ★ ★ ★ April 29, 2024

this book is all around us it's a deep message about blood relation are not the only relationship between humanity is also I like about thik book is that it's a basic need to know my opinion is that if this book is showed in your display it's a direction to make way to dreams and take risks . every line has meaningful. it's a worth to read maybe it's helpfull for me in future. I will highly recommend this book . maybe I found a book like this in future. thank you

Did you find this helpful? Yes No

M   Mike Angelo Rapio

★ ★ ★ ★ ★ September 16, 2023

It is a life changing book that I have ever read, sorts of emotions came to my mind. I was motivated after reading it. I got sad for reading it. But the most important thing I learned about it was these are all life experiences that we have to go through with our journey. Some may be a good experience or a bad one, but what's more important than that is we learned from them, we acquire new knowledge from those experience that changes our lives and if someday we would have to face the same situation, we know what to do and make things better.

H   Huma Deshmukh

★ ★ ★ ★ ★ November 18, 2023

one of the best book ..... with simple English...helpful...I really enjoy and learn from it ...

Did you find this helpful? Yes No

S   Saini Manish

★ ★ ★ ★ July 3, 2024

Such an inspirational book and makeing clear vision towards our goals. I felt very clear in my own path after i read this book. Its mostly helps people who suffers from self doubt , work stress , and being engaged through there own thoughts.

Did you find this helpful? Yes No

Preface

Break Free from Social Anxiety—Starting Today! 🚀

Social anxiety silently holds millions back, limiting potential and clouding daily life. But it doesn't have to be this way. This book uncovers every facet of social anxiety—from its root causes to the emotional toll it takes—while providing a clear, psychological roadmap to freedom.

In the final chapter, you'll discover **five powerful strategies** to overcome social anxiety. Follow them for just one month, and you'll witness a **remarkable transformation** in your confidence and interactions. Fear is nothing more than an illusion, and your willpower is stronger than you think.

This is not just another self-help book—it's a **proven, practical guide** to reclaiming your confidence. **Make the promise to yourself today—start reading, start changing!** 💪 📖

Contents

Digital Overdose

(Image Source:- https://www.pexels.com/photo/heart-and-zero-neon-light-signage-2694434/)

Despite all the technical developments, humans connect in a fraction of a second. But the sad part is that today's digital gazette usage separates many people. Let us see what this digital overdose has done to our society in the last decades. People nowadays are addicted to digital overdoses as it is part of their lifestyle. From waking up in the morning to bedtime, this digital overdose is dominating our lifestyle.

One of the most significant disadvantages is that it grabs our social skills like seeing, observing, hearing, talking, listening, and feeling other people, which is a big disaster. It creates a gap between human interactions. People are becoming experts in typing messages rather than interacting. Neighbors will never see another neighbor. Kids nowadays are addicted to digital games. Youths are addicted to adult shows. People compare their social status to their digital status. Not getting likes may increase anxiety. Many are suffering from screen time disease. At this time, our attention span is reduced to one-minute reels. We become looser every day by losing our concentration and memory power.

After all this, one question we have to ask ourselves. Who is making a profit out of these?

If the mobile phone is the problem, then you may also question me: why am I selling this ebook here if that is the case?

No, the root cause of all the problems is in our minds.

Interactions and sharing things are basic needs of humans. Don't try to stop them. As a 90's kid, I remember my childhood days with my friends. How do we enjoy in the ground? The whole day, we used to interact with family and friends. Those days are golden. I often question myself: where did that old-school interaction go? Why are we becoming addicted to devices?

It made me interact with different personalities. Many ideas I exchanged. I felt myself very light and tension-free. That day, I realized humans are built to interact and share things. If we stop doing that, it will create many problems. You don't believe it, but I have many topics to interact with, even with an unknown person. It built my confidence. Whatever job we do, interacting with the opposite person and knowing about him/her is good. This skill can make us very unique personalities.

"Just decide to talk, then you will realize you have plenty of thoughts to share. "

Don't Forget that We are Social Beings.

(Image source:- https://www.pexels.com/photo/boys-on-the-soccer-field-wearing-white-uniforms-10347868/)

Observe the nature of how the creator made it. Everything is interdependent. Trees will give us fresh oxygen and accept our carbon dioxide. If a cow eats the leaves of trees, cow dung will be used for the growth of trees. Food that is waste for us will also be food for other organisms. You may now understand the pattern that nature built us. There is a 'recycling system' for each thing surrounded by us. Everyone is interdependent. We can call this an ecosystem as well.

In the same way, we are interdependent on society as well. It may be your classmate, colleague, neighbor, relative, family, or loved one. We depend on them, and they rely on us. It is a fact, and we have to accept it. We have to nourish our bonds to better society.

I want to give one example of mine. I was introduced to video games on TV in 2005 as a kid. I can't explain how happy I was with those video games. I used to play it day and night. After some days, I used to notice that I was unhappy to play. We can play a maximum of 1 hour of video games, but it will slowly create stress in our minds—strain our eyes, and tension in our daily lives. However, I never experienced this kind of stress, strain, or tension while playing outdoor sports with my friends. I played cricket the whole day with my friends during the summer holidays. I have never faced such difficulties while playing with my friends. I did not notice that difference as a kid, but if I think about it now, I can list many.

- Mainly the interaction with my friends.
- Physical exercise while playing.

- The fresh air and fun chats kept my stress level low.

- There are a lot of things to learn from other friends.

- Learning about building a team.

If I list, I will still list as many as possible. But again same video games; I also played with my friends, which was stressless. You may also experience it many times. Playing video games will drain your mental power, but playing outdoor sports will enhance your mental power. So, we built to social interactions. We are built to share our things, and no technology is there to replace humans.

However, modern science and technology produce so many gazets to entertain us. It may be mobile phones or even cars which we will use daily. I am not against it; technology is always there to uplift us, but we must know how to use it. It should be like a pickle to our meal. There are many other aspects in life to which we have to taste. Understanding this, we are masters of those gazets, not the servants of those. We are gifted with enormous energy of which we are not aware. The treasure is hidden within; you only need the correct password.

Don't Ever Think Everybody is Focusing on You.

(Image source:- https://www.pexels.com/photo/man-in-black-framed-eyeglasses-eating-pizza-4728859/)

It starts like this: when you go to a party, marriage function, or other social gathering. You will restrict yourself to talk or interact with other people. It will be caused by many thoughts that we have thought wrongly. For example, if we see an attractive personality at parties, we start comparing ourselves to them.

Many people think they are not attractive by their looks. It happened to me as well. I was overweight in my college days, and you don't believe that was the primary reason for me not interacting with many people. At that time, I was very conscious about my body, and I always had a worthless perspective in my mind about me. I always thought that if I became close to some people, they would make fun of me. I used to compare myself with attractive physical personalities and rated myself with respect to them. I avoided the crowd, so gradually, people stopped interacting with me. I felt so bad, and I was depressed for many days. See, nobody can read our minds. These puzzles are only created in our minds, and if people know that I am avoiding them for this reason, they might have come to me. But they don't know the cause and think I am avoiding them.

At that time, one new admission to our college came from another city. I used to observe him, and he was overweight more than I was. However, he was the most attractive personality in our entire college. He participated in every sport, including dance, skit, etc. More people want to spend time with him. He used to talk so nicely with everyone. He used to make fun of himself before anybody would do. He was appointed as our class leader and became the favorite student of our teachers within 6 months. He loves to interact with people, he loves to make more friends, and he has many connections. Everybody will ask about him when he has not come for such social gatherings. I got his motivation to build my personality as well. I realized now, "I am not I, but I am every tiny part of my surroundings made me. From childhood to adulthood, we learn and adopt many things from our surroundings. Today, I am nothing without my surroundings. "

Why am I telling this?

As my beloved friend inspired me, I got inspired by many other human beings around me. We get good things from others and should adapt to grow ourselves. From then I transformed myself to talk with everyone and shaped my identity within the crowd. You may have many reasons to avoid crowds, but stick to one that will give you hope of positivity. Great leaders know this and will build their personality by observing society.

Stay Away from Toxic People.

(Image source:- https://www.pexels.com/photo/woman-with-face-paint-with-pumpkin-3038246/)

Sometimes, we will be struck by the surroundings of toxic people. We feel that they are poisonous and uncomfortable for us, and still, we listen to them. The people who want to hurt you will find many ways. They know the ways to hurt you. It means you also allowed those ways to open for them to hurt you. Understand this: we should not blame the world because of toxic people. Because of those 10 people, why should we suffer? Why do we lock ourselves in a room? Why miss the happiness that the world created? Why should we be unhappy?

You may believe that the whole world is criticizing and blaming you. The fact is only those 10 toxic people are doing it since they surround you, and it becomes the world for you. For example, an ordinary person can only interact with a maximum of 50 people daily. It may be five members from your family, five members from your neighbor, five members from shopkeepers and other workers, 25 members from the office/workplace, five friends, and five strangers. It may be minimum or maximum according to different people. What else, and that is repeated for the rest of the days? You are rotating between these 50 people every day.

You think you are living for these 50 people around. You are taking tension and stress from those people. You are worried about these people's words. Understand this: no one will help in your hard times, and those who support you are those who understand you. You should give preference to those people who support you. Others may say different things about you, but it should not bother you. Those people are not even in your circle. You are living for your satisfaction. The moment you start to please others, everyone will say everything. It's hard to listen to all. You have to listen to your inner voice. You should know what is correct for you. You should learn to be happy without causing tension to others. That's it. Nothing matters to you.

Maybe in those 50 people, you will get to 10 toxic people. I understand this. Leave those 10 people and search for another person who matches your vibe. May the 11th person become your best friend for your life. I don't know. The universe has blessed us with unlimited energy, and we suffer in the limited things. Every day, ask for unlimited. Expand your boundaries. See what great leaders and celebrities will do. They want to make more connections and save the best they have now. If you don't like the people around you, switch to like-minded people you like. These people are also around you. For example, if you want to play badminton, go to where people play badminton, and you get everyday things to play. This choice is still there for you; don't forget it.

There are many types of people around you. The people who want to make friends only if the other person has the same habits(or like-minded) as them. Some people may make friends even if they have a 50% match in between. Some people will initially open up themselves, and some people will not. They wait till they understand you. However, some common points should be to interact and talk with others. Without these common points, people may not show interest.

That's why how to talk to a stranger is a skill. That is not easy for every person. We should have more knowledge to interact with and know strangers. That comes with experience only. Experience means we have to explore more people than we already know. On the bus, you can meet a person beside you. While walking in the park, you may be seeing some people. You get some people while taking things in the shop, and there is no scarcity. The people are there all over the globe. One thought should spark in our mind to interact with them. This spark will itself do magical things.

Pets are Great Healers.

(Image source:- https://www.pexels.com/photo/two-yellow-labrador-retriever-puppies-1108099/)

I bought a puppy from the street in my childhood days. At first, my parents became angry with me. I promised them that I would take care of that puppy. Many days over, you don't believe everybody in my family got attached to that puppy so strongly. Because of that puppy, everybody in our family was happy. Seeing a few minutes, what that puppy does is a healing for our whole stressful day. Still, I will be seeing this kind of puppies or cat videos on YouTube; there were many views on those channels. That indicates that people love those moments with their pets.

I will tell you the real story of a girl who lived near our village. She was very frustrated and used to be sad all the time. She had no friends, and she used to quarrel with everyone. Her main thing is her expectations; she was always sad about her expectations not being fulfilled. Humans always want control over our situation, but it is not always possible. Sometimes, we need only one best person to share things. When that person is also not in our life, our heart breaks. The girl's father magically brought a new calf to the house that year. She was given to take care of that calf. She used to feel happy after seeing that calf, and slowly, she started talking with that calf. It is almost 10 years, and she used to share everything with that cow. Everyone thinks she is a mad girl, but it doesn't bother her. She believes animals have the purest feelings towards us, and she will get relief after sharing happy or sad things with those animals. She believes that the cow is her best friend.

I understood that time like, "We always need one being which belongs to us, and we belong to that being." This feeling is incredible. You will also start sharing your stories with trees when you believe this. I saw some people who care and talk with trees. I even saw some people talk with their favorite vehicle and will give it a nickname. After all, we are social animals and love the things around us. See, it is all our feelings, and it is in the purest form. We don't have expectations, and we unknowingly fulfill our things. We don't become angry about what our pets or trees or anything did to us. We don't even expect anything from them. It is the purest form of love—this form of love we must cultivate with humans as well. You can see around you that the toxicity of any relationship depends on their unrealistic expectations towards each other. However, I am not talking about dependency. Dependency will bind two people. You will be depending on some other things which you will not expect. For example, a husband knows to clean the garden, and a wife knows to cook well, or vice versa. It is a dependency they have; it will bind them. However, unrealistic expectations are like the expectations you think in your mind and the opposite person doesn't even get to know. The taste of both the persons may differ, and what came to your mind may not come to his mind. We have to move towards an understanding mindset. We have to study that person and try to understand him/her. Try to understand his/her mind. Both should cultivate this mindset. We have to move ourselves to a fulfilled life.

Surrender Your Anxiety.

(Image source:- https://www.pexels.com/photo/baby-sleeping-with-animal-plush-toy-2797865/)

Imagine those days when you were kids. You never thought about this society. You are a free bird in this universe, and you always love to do things that you love. There was no fake smile or fake happiness you experienced. You were honest from inside and outside as well. You play, tire, eat, and believe—the belief in security with your parents. You slept in their hands peacefully, forgetting everything around you. That was the state of no stress or no anxiety. We have to achieve this state now, and it is not difficult. "Learning many things may make us intelligent, but unlearning some things will make us wise."

Nowadays, whatever you are seeing is not valid. It is just an illusion created by your brain. It is like you are locking the doors inside the room and shouting for help. But you locked it and know how to unlock it. All this started from inside, and you have all the strength to unlock it or to break that door. If you feel it is impossible, don't believe it is not real. You can do one last thing if you feel it is real. Surrender that to your protector, whom you believe. Many believe that God, nature, work, energy, science, etc. I don't know what you think. Relax your mind and concentrate on its calmness. Take your mind to a peaceful world and meditate there for a few minutes. If it is impossible, calmly and peacefully talk with your protector. Express your happiness, sadness, worries, thankfulness, and so on to your protector and ask for his/her help in achieving it. Do this at least one minute a day; if you feel good, you can stretch it for long.

This question of whether or not it exists is another topic of discussion. I will not talk about those things. Some things we can only feel, and those will not be able to explain because they are above our sense organs.

Surrender your pain, stress, anxiety, tension, pressure, and all the negative things to your protector. There is no one positive than the protector you are seeing. Surrender everything to him/her just like a cup of dirty water is thrown into the ocean. Not only will it accept your negative thoughts, but it will also fill your mind with positive thoughts. Believe that protector, sleep like a baby in his/her hands. There is nothing more beautiful than this in the world. Surrender your anxiety and recharge your mind.

I don't know how you will get recharged. Some people go to spiritual places to charge, some people meditate, some people go on holiday trips, some people will work more if they are passionate, some people will help the poor, some people will spend time in nature, some with family, some with alone, and some don't want to do anything. I don't know which way is yours.

It has been many days, while you are doing many things, but few hours don't do anything. It's a state of your mind to clear noise. Just observe. Just go into nature, observe your surroundings, and observe everything calmly. It is an incredible power within us. Many powerful people did this, and all inventions took this route. There is nothing in this world as you imagined. Come out of it and try to find the reality. The reality is this world is the mirror. The whole world will act as you act. You act as the entire world. The trick is you can change the whole world by changing you.

You may ask where to change it.

If 10 people are complaining about you differently, don't worry, but if 10 people complain the same thing about you, then it's time to change. Adjusting to people's mindset is very difficult. If nature is giving this hint, then don't miss this opportunity. Grab it first.

We have to make some sacrifices, and I can say it is the filter we must place in front of us to be liked by people. It is the process of looking inside me and eliminating the things troubling people to become close to us. It is not where we should think about our ego, but it should be for love to all. It will happen only when you surrender yourself to your protector.

Humans are Not that Much Complicated.

We think humans are the most complicated beings. My reading friends, it is not like that. Yes, I agree that some people are foolish. They can't be good at everything. Humans put their energy and efforts where they can get good results. It can be anything. It can be work, sport, exercise, business, relationships, entertainment, etc.

It is purely a personal aspect. Which thing may appear suitable may not appear for the next minute. Our surroundings will influence us also. It can also be age-dependent. Age below 15 may be lost in playing, ages between 17 and 25 will be lost in building a career, ages between 26-35 will be lost in finding a better partner, age in between 35-55 will be lost in finding becoming better parents and age 55-70 will be lost in maintaining health and spiritual things, after that, everything is a bonus. Age is the primary factor driving our lives, and it is one example

I gave for a better understanding. Many aspects will affect human beings like this, but we don't know which person will indulge in which thoughts. What is important to them right now? What makes them happy right now? Where is 100% focus present right now?

We can't predict. For example, an unpopular, dedicated scientist may look like a fool in society. Just because he will give more time and energy to his work, he is unaware of many things that happen in society. If I try to make him understand the values system regarding society, that eminent scientist will think I am the biggest foolish creature on earth. I am not criticizing anyone here. That is common in every conversation we have. So, that scientist will deny me and not want to talk with me further because I am unsuitable for his ideology. It is the same thing I will do to anyone opposing my ideology.

The point is every human likes to be happy and appreciated in this society. Everyone can't be perfect at everything we do. Understanding this, we must target the topics in which we are mutually interested. See the social media apps; they know the psychology of humans. They spent millions of dollars learning human psychology. Because they know every penny they invest is worthwhile in the long run. That's why you will find mutual friend requests, likes from your friend posts, and so many. They target like-minded people. Conforming with people is not so hard if you know what makes them happy. These conversations will continue for a long time and improve the bond between two humans. At least in this aspect, we should accept we humans are selfish. I accept myself as a greedy creature. I am not a monk, and I respect a monk's selflessness for the betterment of the world. But when we are in society, I believe in positive selfishness, which gives me happiness, and I can give happiness to society. At least this selfishness will keep two people happy and build a positive atmosphere around them. It is a win-win situation for both who are living in a society.

That means I am not suggesting you break your character and do acting. It should be a genuine act; otherwise, it will not last long. It will damage you more than the previous one. It should be like part of you, and this should be like an update for your character.

Everyone loves the positive character if we accept them in the right way.

Thoughts are the Source.

(Image source:- https://www.pexels.com/photo/mental-health-related-conceptual-art-8378723/)

Understanding people is not easy, and learning will take a lot of time. There are so many varieties of people we meet every day.

It may be language, culture, thinking, and behavior. You name it, and we will see different varieties of people every day. Understanding them is a difficult task.

I suggest you show up every day. The majority of issues happen because of misunderstandings. It doesn't matter if you misunderstand somebody today, then show up tomorrow. Try to understand him/her. Think calmly and peacefully. Some situations will create anger within us, but some situations may also create pleasantness. Observe those thoughts and study them.

If you see a person, you may get angry. What is the thought behind that anger? Is it his/her mistake? Is it tolerable? Does it include your mistake as well? Is it because of the eco clash? Why was it generated in your mind? Why is it fueling your emotions to it?

Imagine if you hate someone and don't talk with him/her. When you see him/her, hundreds of thoughts will be generated in your mind. Those thoughts are neither pleasing to you nor to him/her. It will create negative energy, which may cause people to repeal each other. It will create stress and tension in your mind and the opposite person. You are not only harming him/her, but you as well. It will exponentially increase as time increases. If it is with one person you see daily (such as a colleague), it is also intolerable stress in your mind. If it becomes 10 people, then I don't discuss the consequences. It may be terrible, and that person will think 100 times about stepping out of his/her home.

Our inner world creates 80% of problems, and the remaining 20% of existing issues are curable. We must control our inner world first and stop thinking negatively about every situation. If your eyes see an opposite person as a villain every day, how come he/she can become a hero/heroine in your life? They will be hero/heroine for those who see them like that. Give people better thoughts, and they will try to match you. Observe your thoughts and emotions, and follow your thoughts. That's why a relationship is too complex to handle. It is like a glass cup. It is delicate, and it needs extra care and effort to survive. Only a calm and patient mind will make the happy surroundings around it. That is a personal choice.

"Winning hearts is more important than winning quarrels. The heart, once won, is forever won. Focus your energy here."

Setting Boundaries is Crucial.

I want to imagine that the relationship between humans will evolve with time. I depicted the Closeness Vs. Time graph to get an understanding of the two best possible cases. Many cases exist, but I took the best maximum and minimum cases.

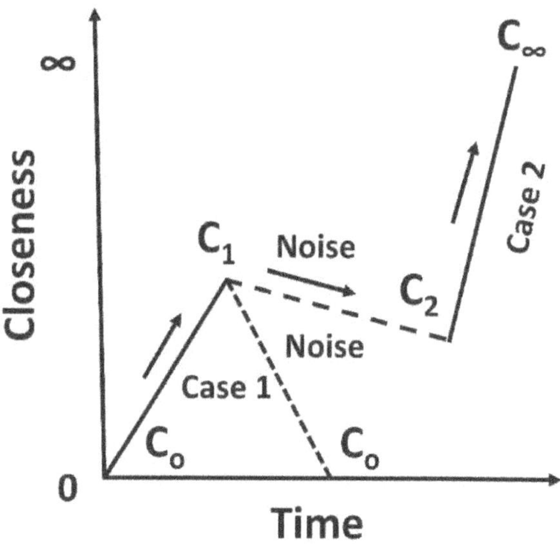

Case 1:- Path of C_o-C_1-C_o

It is the worst case you can imagine. Two people become close (C_1) after some time, and their understanding worsens (C_0).

Case 2:- Path of C_0-C_1-C_2-C_∞

It is the best possible case for people's closeness. Here, people become close (C_1), and at the next level, people's understanding will worsen again. But here, the two people want their relationship to be strong. They nourish and give their best to strengthen those bonds to reach 'C_2'. After this stage, they will get very few disputes or quarrels and reach the C_∞ stage, where their closeness is infinite.

Important stage (C_1-C_2)

Stage C_1-C_2 is called the "Noise stage." It is the stage where your energy needs to be more. Here, most of the misunderstanding happens. It may be a real person who is meeting another real person. It leads to friction. Till now, you liked the person who knows how to act well, or we can say we meet the outer ring of a person. This outer ring differs from a person's body language, which may relate to his profession, work, or other things. It is needed for every human being as a shielding layer to protect themselves. It is natural in every human being. It is either good or bad to discuss. The first few days you met are not the real ones. The real person may come out as time goes on.

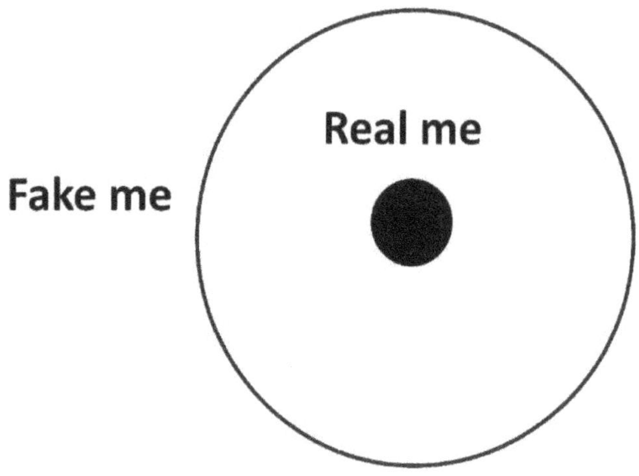

Here you can see the noise stage (C_1-C_2). The behavioral and psychological ways they treat you will have too many ups and downs. It is the stage where you must tune the frequencies to admit to the opposite person.

Many people think about good and bad here. I suggest that there is no good or bad, but there is a match and a mismatch. For example, a non-alcoholic person will not like the person of alcoholics. It is entirely personal. But if both people are alcoholic or non-alcoholic, they have the best company. The individual decides to tolerate another person. It depends on many other factors as well. This stage is uncertain, and people struggle to match their frequencies. But my friends, it is both people's willpower to elevate this relation to the next level, "C_∞."

One more thing is essential here. That is to draw clear boundaries with each other. Say, for example, you like to dance, which makes you happy. The friend of yours should not deny that and not to force you to stop that. See, that is your personal choice, and you must discuss it with them beforehand. The same applies to you as well, and you have to give the same freedom to that person for his/her likes. See, when we love someone, the most valuable gift we can give to those is trust and freedom. There is nothing more precious than those. In some cases, it is better not to get close to some people, and it will indulge toxic thoughts in you. You feel them often, and those toxic thoughts will make you suffer. And what are toxic thoughts? It is purely personal. There should be no regrate or no worries. It is your personal choice to continue a relationship with other people. But don't make life miserable. You should be happy in life. "It is better to be happy with one person than miserable with 100 people."

Question yourself often about continuing or discontinuing those relations. Question yourself also whether you are not the problem for the misunderstanding. These types of interrogation will lift both personalities.

Because of one spoiled mango, we cannot decide all the other mangoes are like that. If you get spoiled mango, then try to find better mangoes. It doesn't mean better mango do not exist.

(Image source:- https://www.pexels.com/photo/men-s-white-button-up-dress-shirt-708440/)

Don't expect too much in any relation. Remember this: we are friends, so we help each other. But we help each other, that's why we are not friends. Materialism or dependency is good, but it should not occupy the core of any relationship. Their only it will fall to 'C_0'. I wish you all that you have to reach the 'C_∞' stage happily with as many as you can. All the best for your journey.

Creating a Friendly Society

(Image source:- https://www.pexels.com/photo/hands-making-a-star-6476771/)

What is society?

It is a group of people. However, groups of people will be formed by like-minded individuals. Nature has given us immense powers, and influencing people is the most powerful. Everyone has the potential to influence his/her surroundings. The only thing is, we have to train our minds to do it. It will not be done in one or two days, but if you consciously train your thoughts, you may see results in a few days—that angle of deviation to the thoughts we have to add daily to our routine. You may be seeing such skills in the person around you. See, observe, and absorb the things from them.

In this digital society, everybody forgets the real interaction. It's time to bring back this.

How is it possible?

It is possible for you. Each one can at least influence 10 people around you. Those 10 people will spread it to 100, and it will compound. It's time to spread positivity around. It's time to become a real-life hero/heroine in some people's lives. It is a core idea to bring back the happy society around you. If not 10 people, start with at least one, then see the impact around you. See the confidence around you. Feel the positive waves around you. Just like the heart circulates blood to the whole body to make it alive, it is your turn to make the society around you live.

How will it be achieved?

It is a simple process. Eliminate fear and replace it with thoughts of courage while seeing the people. You know why I am saying this. People love courageous ones. They like your confidence more than the subject you are telling them. 9 out of 10 don't know the subject, but they are actually seeing your confidence. Do you understand this? See the leaders around you. It is happening all around you. Just say with confidence.

In this digital world, winning people by fundamental interactions is very easy. Many people are craving for real interactions. Many people want their real friend to share their things. Believe me, it's hard to get in this digitally indulged world. I am not against anyone and any products. I am saying it's time to encash it, but if not, don't think about any other day.

5 practical tips to achieve this:-

1. While praying to God, add, "I love people around me. I want to initiate a positive atmosphere around me. Make people interact with me. I want to make them happy around me. Please give me the power, courage, and strength to make this change. Please give me that righteousness to guide my way. Let all of us spread positive waves around."

2. Dream every night before sleeping like you are talking with every person you meet. You surround everyone, and they are happy with your presence. You touched everyone's heart with your words—everyone's face blossomed like a flower with a smile.

3. Saying "Hi," smiling at everyone, or wishing "Good morning" face to face consumes much less energy, but it will build strong connections. Don't ever miss it.

4. Be a good listener. Interact with them, "How are you, sir/madam?", "Is everything right?" "You are looking sad today" and "What is the reason for your happy mood?" Crack jokes without hurting them. Everyone wants to be happy in life. Everyone wants that smiling face to interact with them. No one came to the earth to be dead serious. It's all they do not get the better company. This type of conversation will make everyone know that humanity is not dead. Yes, caring and at least listen what they are

suffering. Give suggestions or help if possible. It will make an unbreakable bond with you, and they will return it one day.

5. People love to be praised. Genuinely praise them for their good thing. At least that is the recognition they need for their good things. It will fuel their motivation to do those positive things.

Social anxiety is just a fear of people. It has nothing to do with reality. I challenge people to do these 5 points only and consistently for a month. Start with five people around you and then see the magic it does. You don't believe you have such a miraculous power within you. As you are a source, everything will change. I am not kidding or simply giving those 5 points. It worked for me in my college days. Everybody was surprised by this change in me. Being an introvert to an extrovert is such a fabulous journey for me. I realized that some people would want to listen to me at that time. Some people like me, and the beauty is they are around me. I am blessed to have such a positive atmosphere around me. Now, it's your time, my friend. Spread your arms, and then you will see the many hands around you that will join your journey.

Check Out Other Books by Author

- ✓ If you like this book, follow the author for future updates.
- ✓ Please share this with your loved ones.
- ✓ Please give your honest review for this book and encourage the readership.
- ✓ Don't forget to check out other self-help books by the author.

Thank You

Check Out More Self Help Books by Author

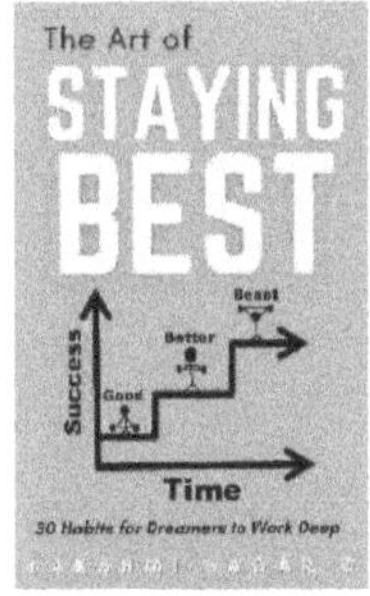